- Create notes and mortgages to yourself as a lien against your property and then use them as down payments on other properties.
- Sell your house, thereby receiving the full equity. Part may be used to move into another house with the balance going to investments.
- Trade your property for other property.

Any lending institution can help you prepare these documents. That's the easy part. The hard part is making the decision to go ahead. And before that decision is made, several other things need to be considered.

Must Be a Good Investment

The first consideration of purchasing any property should be its investment qualities. I have said this so many times. Yes, it's important to look at the tax implications, but your first analysis should be to determine if it's a good investment or not.

Now the opposite is true when selling. If you're planning on trading or selling your house, take special note. The first consideration when selling is to determine the tax ramifications. It's amazing how quickly selling one property affects your tax status on other property.

You'll need to set the sale of any one property in context with the others. Write it all out. See how the properties you're holding, and thus creating tax write-offs, will affect the sale. See if your proceeds will be used to leverage you into yet another property that may create tax write-offs this year to offset your gain.

Isn't investing exciting? All of these great things to do to get ahead and keep all of your money working for you.

The Laws of Leverage

Making small amounts of money do large amounts of work is a main ingredient to successful investing.

We all talk about this but unless it becomes an integral part of our investing philosophy then this successful law is wasted.

Once you master it though, you realize that you don't need as much money as previously thought. You can demand less out of your house and yet get this lower amount to do more.

If you look at others and think back on your own investing career, were not the best deals made when you were broke? Poor people make great investors.

People with money have a tendency to spend it to solve problems. It's the easy road. And then, once this large amount of money is tied up into the property, the property takes charge. It's sad to see people doing things they don't want to do just to free up their money once again.

One more point: once a large amount of money is tied up, people have a tendency to over react. They start doing things they normally wouldn't do. This is called being emotionally involved. Usually the higher the emotional level, the lower the intellectual level. If you find yourself in this position, seek competent help so you will at least be getting some feedback and hopefully build a foundation of contrasting opinions upon which you can base your decision.

It is easy to make the laws of leverage work for you—pretend that you are poor!

Try a Little First

It is like a revelation when people realize that they do not have to take out all of their money and yet accomplish a lot.

In reality, it is a relief for them to know that they will not have to commit to a whole new lifestyle because they take out a large loan.

One other important point is that the people can take out a little, test the waters with different types of purchases, and learn what they would do if and when they do get larger amounts.

Sometimes the job of tying up large properties or large amounts of properties seems ominous. But, look at the alternatives.

If you want to put down large down payments, you are going to spend a lot of time getting at the money and maximizing it, investment will be tougher. Time will move on and you will probably spend as much time worrying about it, and when you try to sell, more time trying to free it back up.

On the other hand, if you use very little cash on the downside, granted the time needed to find the good deals will be more, but two important good points come to mind:

(1) That is time spent with no commitments. You are free to look, to explore, to negotiate; and most important, you are free to change your mind.

(2) Because very little of your money is tied up you are in control when it is time to dispose of the property. You are free to sell it or trade it any way you please.

Many people feel that if small amounts are good, big amounts must be better. Maybe so, but, maybe not. Along with holding large amounts of money comes a large responsibility. Carefully weigh the amount of time you are willing to spend to manage your money effectively.

Creating Tax Write-Offs

Now that we have covered leverage and other aspects of the decision making process of freeing up equity for investment capital, it is time to cover a few basic pointers in maximizing your efforts.

The following list will point the way to several things you should consider. It is by no means complete. It is offered here to help you see several things that could and should be done.

- Learn as much as you can about the new tax law (The Recovery Act of 1981). Get a functional knowledge of:
  - (a) the new write-off schedules
  - (b) the different types of property that may be a part of any real estate purchase
  - (c) Section 179 property
- Study up on carrybacks and carryovers so you can see how one year's actions affect other years. Be acutely aware of the dates which represent the one year mark for long term capital gain purposes.
- Consider selling your property on installments to avoid large tax liabilities.
- Make sure that you have an up-to-date financial statement.
- Work up a system for having some sort of P&L (Profit and Loss) Statement so you can quickly pinpoint things to do and alternatives for solving problems.
- Become more familiar with the terminology of your transactions so you will know what you are committing yourself to.
- Develop and maintain a good record keeping system. Put special emphasis on doing what it will take to effectively do your taxes next year.
- Develop terminology that will let you take the maximum tax write-offs on each purchased property.

A Little More Detail

Let's take a little extra time here and cover this last point in more detail. When you buy an average rental property, part of the purchase may include items that can be written off faster.

For example: a $100,000 four-plex may be valued at $90,000 for the building and $10,000 for the land. According to the old system, this would produce about $5,000 in depreciation expense which will offset exactly that much in profits and gains from other sources.

By breaking the purchase price down even further, we can value the stove, refrigerator, dishwasher and separate air conditioning unit (all 5-year types of property) at $2,000. Then we can put a valuation on the carpet, drapes, furniture at $8,000 (this is a 3-year type of property). Now taking these new figures and couple it with the new write-off schedules and the average deduction will jump from $5,000 to about $9,000.

What a great advantage this is in and of itself. It could be thousands of dollars in actual savings, and added to similar write-offs on other properties, the savings could make for a very nice tax liability situation.

The following phrase could be used in every purchase you make, and even if you plan on selling the property, things happen to alter the plans, so make it a part of every offer.

"The valuation of the different types of property of this purchase price will be established between the buyer and the seller before closing."

You may then write down the values of each of these types of property and make it a part of the closing documents. Make sure both the buyer and the seller sign it. These values may be established by an independent appraiser. If that route is used the clause above could read:

"The valuation of the different types of property of this purchase price will be established by an independent appraisal. The cost of this appraisal will be paid by ____________."

Now that this is done, the tax calculations are relatively simple. The IRS form has you just list the values placed on these different units. The savings are tremendous for such little effort.

Problem Solving

This following section will explain a step-by-step procedure for solving problems. The concept explained may be used on all sizes of problems. Let's use a small problem to see how it works.

Let's say we have a duplex that has a $100.00 a month negative cash flow. We want to make it break even so it won't cost us anything out of our pocket. We do not want to sell it.

Step 1: **Look to the property itself.** Is there anything we can do to raise the income or lower the expenses?

Step 2: **Look to other property that we own.** Is there anything we can do to raise the income and/or lower the expenses on any of our other properties. Note: Lowering expenses for step 1 and step 2 could involve renegotiating the debt service (monthly payments) on existing loans.

Step 3: **Look to new property.** Could we purchase other property with a positive cash flow? (Other rentals or even discounted mortgages.) Could we buy and sell on contract a piece of property which would then provide a positive cash flow with very limited tax liabilities?

Step 4: **Look at your tax situation.** Is there anything we can do to maximize our tax write-offs on not only this property, but others as well to free up money that would be going to the I.R.S.? This step involves using steps 1, 2 and 3 within itself. It also includes looking at two other ideas: (a) check your W-2 status. Are you claiming all the dependents you are entitled to claim? (b) Keep better records. How many small items do you buy to handle your rental units, how many tanks of gas are used up, and how many other expenses are paid without being properly posted so they can be written off?

Step 5: **Look to yourself.** Is there anything else that you can do to earn more or spend less?

Step 6: **Look to others.** If all else fails and the situation justifies it, look to banks or partners for help.

These steps should be worked in this order. Yes, they can often be used in conjunction with each other. The basis for establishing priorities is found in these steps. If followed they will open up many doors as your mind expands and you get good at conceptualizing blockbusting solutions.

Rome Was Not Built in a Day

Do not let yourself live under the conception that you will make a million by the end of the week. Thinking that way is a misconception.

Build your fortune one brick at a time. Surround yourself with others who can help. Move cautiously and then only after exploring several alternatives.

Remember, your investments will have to stand the test of time. Almost all of what you do will pass to your family (estate) with few hitches if it is handled properly. If you think about this for a minute, two other points become clear:

(1) The fact that you have done things properly to outlast you means that if you are ever disabled or laid up, your affairs will be easy to manage.

(2) And even if nothing drastic happens to you, if things are done right, it will free up your time from putting out fires so you can spend your time the way you want.

You do not have to confront uncomfortable memories down the road. Stop, take a look around, and invest your time and energy in doing things right.

Because investing in real estate is so profitable, the tax implications need to be taken into account at every step.

Do not wait until April 14 to figure out what and how you have done. *Plan your work, then work your plan.*

Skinning the Cat

If this chapter does nothing but stimulate your thinking process it will be a success. The fine points are nice to know but sometimes realizing things in a general way will help just as much, because our only limitation is our lack of imagination.

Knowing this, we are free to explore alternatives. Knowing this also gives us the confidence to seek out professionals and then ask them pertinent questions. It is good to learn from our mistakes, but much wiser to learn from the mistakes of others.

In short, there are many ways to skin a cat and there are many ways to achieve your investment goals.

Ramifications

Nobody wants to spend his whole time stamping out fires, but far too often this is what many investors spend their time doing.

Make sure you take time to do things right. Surround yourself with competent people to help you through problem areas.

It is sad to see people worrying and fretting so much

over problems that could have been avoided or solved by a little forethought.

It is important for all of us to realize that we are the only ones who control our future. Do not expect everything to go right. Murphy is everywhere and the only way to beat him is to be a step ahead of him. A step ahead where we can plan for the unexpected and take the necessary precautions to keep everything going in the right direction.

Publisher's Note

We would like to make a special offer to those of you who have purchased this book.

Many of you will not be able to attend the seminar that Mr. Cook teaches around the country. This is one of the best and most exciting seminars taught and we would like to give you a sampling of what it is like to be there. We have a free tape which is about one hour long that will, in lecture format, cover all these concepts of buying, holding, and selling properties. All the way down to the 3 Entity Approach which is the Z, or the retirement portion of Mr. Cook's whole system of investing in real estate.

It's yours for the asking, write:

ITP-Free Tape
P.O. Box 1201
Orem, UT 84057

Chapter 15

My Real Estate Agent Loves Me

WHEN I became serious about real estate investing, I felt I needed to surround myself with a more dedicated, up-beat team of professionals. I not only needed people who could put together creative deals for me, but individuals who would be flexible when it came to their own interests.

When my program heated up I was purchasing two to five houses a month. It was hard to continually find houses to fix up and quickly resell. To keep up this volume, the idea to "buy right (low) in order to sell right," became all-important. Often the only thing that stood in the way was the large down payments required to close the deals, because of realtor commissions.

Then I Met Mort

At this time I met an agent named Mort. He was aggressive and had a good business sense. We closed a traditional deal wherein he received the traditional 6 percent comission. We got to know each other pretty well during all the paperwork and I found out he was ready to go on his own as he had just passed his broker exam. At this time though, he had an arrangement where he was paying $300 a month for office expense and used another broker's services—not having to split commissions.

Mort and I went to lunch one day and hashed out an investment strategy. The idea of it was that Mort would find properties for me and then take his commissions on contract. (Actually we used a deed of trust.) The terms of the contract would be that the monthly payments would be one percent repay, meaning that if the commissions were $2,000 the monthly payment would be $20. All notes were to bear an interest rate of 11 percent.

Both of us were reluctant at first. I didn't want to impose on him because I knew how important getting cash would be to running his business. He had the same fears, but took the attitude that he would squeeze in a few deals for me in between his regular activities.

Things Picked Up

Nothing happened for about a week and then he called with several houses to go look at. I made offers on four and two were accepted. His commissions were $2,800 and $4,900 and the next month he started receiving his $28 and $49 checks.

During this time he had one other house close and that kept him going. The second month he found two more houses and then by the end of the month one more came along. The first two closed and his net income picked up by another $95. He needed some cash so he discounted the very first $2,800 note for 60 percent of its face value, netting $1,680. At the end of his second month he had:

- Cash of about $1,800 (from sale of the contract plus the other monthly payments.)
- Equities of $14,400.
- Monthly payments still coming at $144 per month.
- Sold one other house that he had found for me but that I didn't buy (it was too close the next month.)
- Sold one other house to me that would be closing the next month.

Now We're Cooking

Already Mort was taking a second look at this M.O. He put me on the front burner and both of us started cooking. He took me to lunch again for the prime purpose of asking me if I could pick up my purchases to four a month instead of two.

I told him that I would have to close the deals quicker and always get the keys upon acceptance of earnest money (if the properties were vacant). He found a different escrow and title officer that could process the transactions in two or three days. We were in business.

Two days later we looked at eleven properties. I made offers on eight. Mort said that four of the eight were really shaky, but because he was taking his commissions on notes, it left almost all of the down payments free to go to the sellers. He literally plastered together four of the deals.

These eight were all small houses, but still his commissions totaled $25,600, netting another $256 a month.

Activity Breeds Activity

There must be something to the expression that activity breeds activity. It seems that the sheer volume of these transactions created other sales for Mort. He was beating the streets for me and uncovered two other houses that he sold to others that closed within two months.

This happened month after month. Mort sowed and then reaped more than he had ever imagined possible.

By this time a lot of things started happening, so many in fact, that I couldn't keep track of them.

I knew deals that he was putting together for me, but had no idea of all the other properties that he was processing because of these contracts.

I don't know all that he did, but we talked often enough for me to find out the following:

One day he came across four 4-plexes that required $5,000 down. The man wanted Mort to sell them for him. Mort knew a good deal when he saw one and attempted to buy them for himself. The man was a doctor and was to the point of exasperation with the tenants and his managers and seriously wanted to unload them. He would have taken zero down, but he wanted to make sure that his buyer had something to lose if they walked away.

Hence the $5,000. The purchase price was $300,000 which was even below market value. Mort didn't have the $5,000 cash but he sure didn't want this one to get away. He knew too many things could happen with even a two or three day delay. He made an offer to the doctor of $10,000 down, using three contracts (they actually totaled $10,450 when the exact figures were researched).

Mort Used His Head

He told the doctor of his 60 cents on the dollar sale, and also mentioned that the profit portion of the monthly payments from these contracts would be able to be claimed as received. They both agreed and the papers were drawn.

The doctor carried the contract on the balance and Mort now had 16 units which were all full, except one. The doctor had trouble worrying about the places, but not Mort. He moved his wife and himself into the vacant unit, and almost immediately started making over $800 a month off the rents besides the tremendous tax benefits.

His Dream House

The second big thing that happened to Mort happened right after they moved into the 4-plex—he found his dream house. Both Mort and his wife were exhausted from moving, but they would have done anything to get into this house.

Unfortunately, the seller was about as creative as a big bank; the only thing he wanted was cash for his equity and the underlying loan was not assumable in any way, shape or form. It had as many clauses as Macy's at Christmas time.

The only solution was a new mortgage. Things didn't look so good. Mort had everything going against him during the first half of the loan interview. Only a broker for a short time, his income wasn't that steady, and most of all, this savings and loan didn't like real estate agents. He thought he was wasting his time, but then the loan officer started asking about his other assets.

A Change in Atmosphere

He brought out his portfolio of contracts and rentals and paraded them in front of her and the whole atmosphere changed. Remember Mort had only been operating like this for about five months but already his contract and rental equities totaled over $160,000.

The loan officer almost got dizzy turning around so fast! The loan was approved. They moved in a week later.

I didn't mention one other exciting aspect of this deal. The house was worth $125,000. The seller was afraid of the market and also needed to move as his company had already transferred him. He lowered the price to $90,000 for Mort if he could get the deal within a month. It only took three weeks and everyone walked away with a smile.

Trading Contracts

Mort had sold four other houses to me by this time and he took these contracts and traded them on a 12-plex. I don't know all the details. I asked him about it once and he just smiled.

Mort had a knack for finding a good deal, usually in real estate, but sometimes in cars. He found a man with a Mercedes for sale at a price way under value. He wanted $4,000 cash, but took one of Mort's $5,000 contracts instead. Thus he could claim the profit on an installment sale. Mort drove away in a nice Mercedes.

"Creamy" Deals

I know that several times other agents would throw good deals at him because they weren't flexible enough with the agent/broker relations to swing them and in walks Mort and gets the cream. As a matter of fact his activities led him into so many creamy deals he should have opened a dairy. Once in a while he would sell properties that included other agents. If they needed cash for their commissions, he would make arrangements to pay them and take the whole contract himself.

Once in a while all investors run into problems. Mort was sued by a tenant. The matter was solved before any litigation in the courtroom, but $920 was chalked up in lawyer fees. Mort didn't want to pay him in cash so he gave him a $1,400 contract. Everyone was happy.

Mort was now to the point that he started buying contracts. He would find houses for me and try to get those having underlying loans to discount the equity and sell them to him.

One other thing that needs to be mentioned here is that Mort was able to claim his commissions as income as he received it (treated like installment sales). He also received the benefits from some of the contracts as if they were cash as in some of his trades. It was great to see that, even after all his wheeling and dealing, he paid no taxes.

Pioneering the System

Many other agents wanted to get involved with him and with me. They could see the large amount of activity that we were creating. Mort wanted all of this business himself. He felt he had pioneered a new system that others had laughed at. Now he was making good money and he wanted to keep it that way. While his cohorts were running around doing the bidding of banks and government agencies to get one deal closed, he was closing five to six. He felt it was his gold mine and guarded it carefully.

Economic necessity or financing restrictions have posed a real problem and forced some agents to move in this direction. The ones that see the whole picture and utilize this method along with their other activities really stack the deck in their favor. Mort didn't want me to let the cat out of the bag, but it needs to be let out. Creativity indeed has become the by-word.

Parting of the Ways

I don't see much of Mort these days. We've both moved on to bigger and better things. He was doing a lot of traveling, looking at big complexes all over the country the last time that I heard from him.

We both learned a lot from each other. We used to joke about the expression, "If you'll do for two years what most people won't do, you'll be able to do for the rest of your life what most people can't do." He made it come true. He was a dealer that wanted to hold all the cards, and he did. Together we stumbled on a way that let him build up his deck faster than either of us thought possible.

My Real Estate Agent

Now, a year later people ask about Mort's success. His own words sum it up best: "Now, I have a steady income, security, travel and a great financial statement. Had I remained a 'traditional' realtor, I'd still be working 60 hours a week to get a few sales closed. Now I have all the freedom I want."

> "Agents, even if it's coming in in bite size pieces, it's better than what you had coming in yesterday."
>
> BOB STEELE
> REAL ESTATE BROKER AND LECTURER

Chapter 16

The Three Entities

"NECESSITY is the mother of invention." So much of what I accomplished in my early years of investing was done by hit and miss; try, back up and try again method. Sometimes I wondered if I would ever get ahead. Luckily though, the information I needed to continue the process of achieving my goals was also supplied.

As I started having some success in one area, it seems that problems would crop up in other areas. Many a good book was written to get people started investing and give the "how to's" of putting certain deals together. And once in a while these books would show the results of such knowledge and effort. So most often, when I needed information I could go to a book or to a professional and get the specific help I needed.

But it became readily apparent that even after achieving a modest amount of success, I would soon need a comprehensive system of investing in real estate. A system that had solutions to these problems:

- generating and *maintaining* positive cash flows.
- sheltering income through long term installment sales and depreciation expense.

- provide security for the future, because who wants to rely on social security.
- keeping my current income (cash) working for the previous three without being swallowed in the IRS abyss.
- a way of working hard for a while then with relative ease, slow down and with only a small amount of time and energy, direct my assets to beat the heck out of inflation.

Sound like a tall order? It was just that. But I also realized right away that maintaining assets is almost as hard as building them up. So, I had no alternative but to find a plan that works.

Obviously, there is no college class for the real estate investor to go and take. Yes, there are books and seminars available and I encourage reading and taking as many of these as possible. However, what is really needed is more comprehensive than any one or two of these. Don't get me wrong. I'm not putting down attempts to buy with no money down, or the idea of papering your way to millions, or equity participation or any of the other host of strategies that rise and fall in popularity. All of these are good as stepping stones. They should be viewed as tools and it is well known how important it is to have the most modern, up-to-date tool chest possible. Once successful, I wasn't in need of specific techniques, but a whole system.

I've spent these past few paragraphs trying to get us all on the same footing. What will be explained now is an A to Z system for investing in real estate that encompasses these good honest methods and puts them to work for your total financial security.

The Start of the System

I was becoming quite successful with my properties and started worrying about my long and short term tax liabilities. It was to answer this tax question that I started the search to find a "total concept" for my investment.

One lesson I have had to learn too many times was to concentrate my energies on one thing. Many of the popular non-real estate tax shelter ideas weren't good for me. My expertise was growing with small properties and I wanted to capitalize on my knowledge and experience. There was no time to start over in a different field.

I spent a whole afternoon listening to an insurance agent/investment counselor expound the virtues of tax shelter investment opportunities. I tried to find the good. I tried hard. But, when I compared his annual investment returns with even my weekly and monthly returns they couldn't compare. I would do better to keep my money working and just pay the taxes.

He then listened to me for a while. He could see where I had come from and the growth I was having, and he candidly told me I needed a corporate pension and profit sharing plan (hereinafter called the PLAN). Hungry for new information, I pressed him for more. What he told me was almost too good to be true.

Before we get into the specifics of the PLAN, let me first mention that you need to incorporate to establish a PLAN. You can incorporate in your state for $40 to $150 and tack on a few hundred dollars more if you use an attorney. You should be a standard corporation with the right to engage in any type of legal venture. This incorporation is on a state level. Everything else that I'll discuss will be federal.

Some Specifics

As many of you know from reading my books and articles, I had devised a system for finding really good deals, then selling them on a wrap-around basis in an attempt to:

- recover my down payment and fix up costs so I could do it again.
- build up a strong steady net income from turning many properties this way.
- spread out my tax liabilities over the 25 to 30 years of the wrap-around mortgage by claiming my gain on the installment sales method.

This plan worked well and became the income generation part of the whole system. Also, the creation of this part let me (a) move on to a more sure way of protecting my assets, and (b) helped me learn how to invest in several types of properties and transactions.

The Plan

I left his agent's office as excited about what he told me as anything I've ever been excited about. I immediately made an appointment with my attorney to check it all out.

Let me give you the gist of what the PLAN can do so you can see how it fits into the picture.

Once incorporated, you use your corporation to buy and sell properties. It needs to start fresh and go out and make a profit. This can be done by any of the techniques you've learned. It can buy with zero down; it can lease option properties; it can form equity participation agreements; it can assume FHA and VA loans. In short—it can do what you can do. It is a legal entity with a life of its own.

It's easy to get it started. Once done, you just buy properties in the corporation's name. If you are new at this it would be advisable to seek competent, professional help. Do it right so you can avoid headaches later on.

Now that the corporation is operating on its own and making a profit, it can take 25 percent of the money available for wages and put it into the PLAN. What is this "money available for wages?" It's not the net profit that is calculated after taking out the wages. *It is all the money available for wages after subtracting the normal expenses.* For example: let's say your corporation made $80,000 gross by turning six properties this year. Let's say the costs of doing business total $20,000. You now subtract the $20,000 from the $80,000 and that leaves $60,000 available for salaries. Maybe your salary to yourself and a few employees total $45,000. You would think the 25 percent would then be on the $45,000 paid out; but it's more than that. The 25 percent is calculated on the whole $60,000 which comes to $15,000. That's $15,000 that can be put into the PLAN.

This donation to the PLAN becomes an immediate tax write off to the corporation. So now the corporation pays less taxes. As a matter of fact, continuing with the same example, our $80,000 gross income is lessened by the $20,000 expenses, the $45,000 in salaries and the $15,000 in donations to the PLAN. That leaves zero income to the corporation which means *no tax liability*.

More on the Plan

What is the Pension and Profit Sharing Plan? It's a separate legal entity set up and recognized by the IRS for the benefit of the retirement of the employees of your corporation.

It is a trust that is a living, thriving entity. It can do so many things, and the real beauty is that you can be the trustee and control where the money is to be invested.

Where does the money go? It goes into the PLAN's checking or savings account. It is then available for investing. You, as the trustee, decide what types of properties it will buy (or sell). It can buy rentals, fixer uppers, discounted mortgages, lots for developing, or even investing stocks, bonds, gold, or any other business. In short, it can do what you can do, but with one major exception. All of the money in the PLAN can be turned over time and time again. The PLAN can buy and sell and make thousands and thousands of dollars—it can even grow into millions—TAX FREE. The PLAN will never pay taxes.

What happens to this money? It just stays in the PLAN investing or earning interest until you decide to retire. Let's say you turn 44 or whatever age and declare your retirement. You begin to take out $3,000 a month to live on. You will now have to claim that income as it is taken out and claim it in your then current tax bracket. (You'll then need to buy a few rental properties to create enough depreciation expense to even offset this amount.)

I've just given the highlights here. Sound good? It's the greatest tax shelter I've ever seen and the PLAN I've just described (Purchase Money Plan) is the least of the three available. (Defined Benefit and Defined Contribution—ask a Pension and Profit Sharing Plan Administrator for details.)

Three Entities

Over the years I've developed the three entity approach to investing in real estate. The three entities are the corporation, the individual, and the pension and profit sharing plan. Don't let this sound complicated. I firmly believe in keeping things simple. This whole system has simplicity at its core and has a goal of progressing rapidly in the present while setting up a foundation for long term wealth accumulation and retention.

The Corporation's main objective is two-fold. It is the entity that makes profits to (a) pay me a salary, and (b) put the money into the PLAN as a tax write-off. Its income comes from capital gains and interest income generated on the loans (mortgages, deeds of trust, etc.) that you create or buy and then carry. By effectively paying out all of its income, the corporation has no tax liability.

The Individual has a main objective of eating and sleeping comfortably. You and I both need just to live—to pay our bills, etc. With the excess salary received from the corporation, we invest in income producing properties which create the depreciation expense and NOL (net operating loss) to offset this same income (and possibly income in other tax years) thereby not paying any taxes.

The PLAN's goal is to grow at a rate faster than the other two can grow and provide income and security for our future. The PLAN is so exciting, and because this chapter is about how the three work together and not all of the details on any specific entity, I have written extensively on the PLAN in a publication called the *Three Entity Approach to Investing in Real Estate*—which also has a prototype plan that has already been approved by the IRS. See ordering information in the back of this book.

Working Together

Once the three entities are in place (and it could take 2 to 3 months to set them up), you are ready to grow faster than you've ever thought possible. If handled right, none of the entities will have to pay taxes—leaving all of your cash available for more investing. Isn't that exciting? You'll once again feel like you're back in control.

Let's see how they work together on a specific deal. When the earnest money agreement (offer to purchase) is signed, you, as the purchaser, should be, "John D. and Mary J. Doe, husband and wife, or their assigns . . ." Your offers should have this so you can assign the transactions to either the corporation or to the PLAN on or before closing the transaction. You'll not always know which one of your entities should be buying the property and this will give you time to decide.

Which one *will* buy it? That depends on several things. I firmly believe in not leaving money tied up in a property. I don't want my cash to become equity. If the deal requires a down payment and fix up costs, then I want either the corporation or the PLAN to buy it. I turn and sell this type of property and I want the profits (probably short term capital gain) to be in one of these two entities.

Which one of the two should receive the profits? That depends on which one has money at the time, or which one I'm actively working with at the moment. Obviously, I would like to be spending all of my time developing the tax free asset growth of the PLAN, but I need to live so the corporation needs to continue to create an income. Yes, the need to be actively working the corporate assets will go down as it creates more and more steady income, but at the beginning you'll have to look closely at which entity will do the buying.

If the purchase requires little or no money down and very few repairs and has a positive or break even cash flow, then the property is a prime candidate to be held for the long term. I buy this property as an individual.

This lets me (a) take advantage of the depreciation expense, and (b) sell it and take advantage of long term capital gains.

Buying long term rental properties and selling only once in a while keeps my investment status as an investor and not a dealer. The properties that will be turned right away can go under the corporation or the PLAN. A corporation is a dealer anyway, but installment sales treatment will prolong the tax ramifications on almost all of my deals. Please refer to Chapter 9 for details.

As I mentioned before, this is a whole system of growth. The beauty is the *no tax,* rapid growth aspects. And the whole system can be done with any business that you're in. Real estate works so well and is a natural for the three entities because of the income generation attribute, the growth potential, and the tax shelter aspect already there to enhance each of the entities.

And because it is a complete system, any of the entities can use any of the techniques of buying, fix up, holding, and selling of real estate. Indeed, the three entity approach gives new life to many of these techniques. They are the tools you need to start and maintain your own investment system.

Let's put this down graphically so you can see how the entities affect each other.

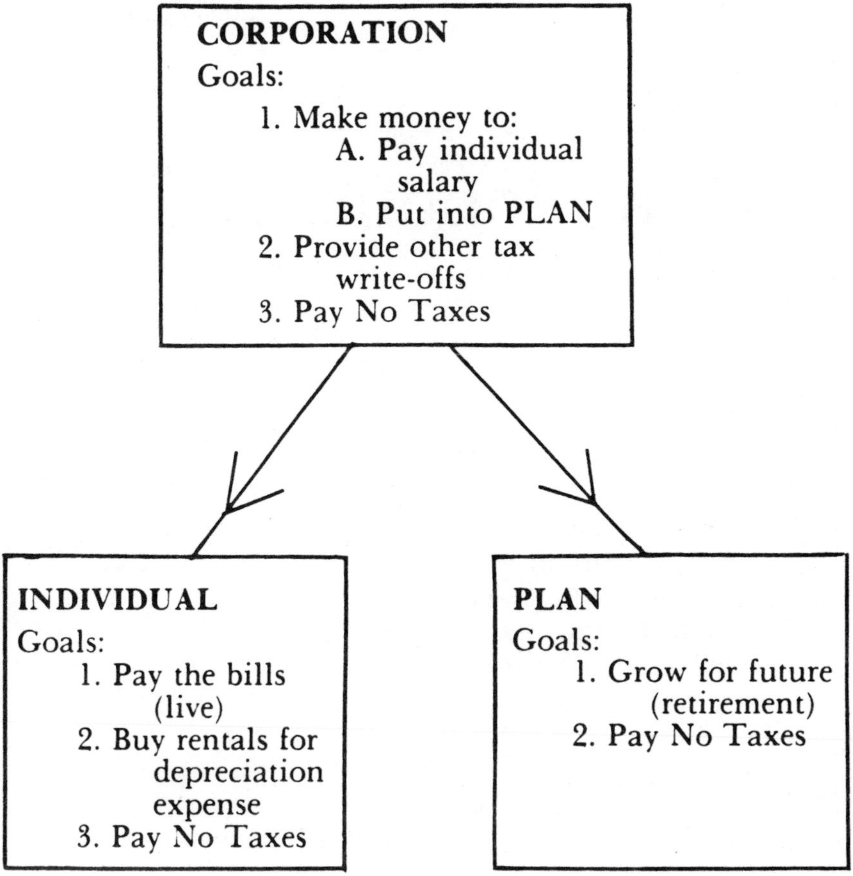

CORPORATION

Goals:

1. Make money to:
    A. Pay individual salary
    B. Put into PLAN
2. Provide other tax write-offs
3. Pay No Taxes

INDIVIDUAL

Goals:

1. Pay the bills (live)
2. Buy rentals for depreciation expense
3. Pay No Taxes

PLAN

Goals:

1. Grow for future (retirement)
2. Pay No Taxes

Chapter 17

Be a Monomaniac

NO BETTER ADVICE could be given than that which says to specialize. After looking at those great men who left their mark in life, one realizes that they targeted their efforts—they were monomaniacs. Thomas Edison once said, "You and I each have eighteen hours doing a number of different unrelated things. I spend it doing just one thing, and some of my work is bound to amount to something."

One of the most famous men to study management—more specifically for our point here, those qualities of management dealing with being effective—had this to say:

> The single-minded ones, the monomaniacs, are the only true achievers. The rest, the ones like me, may have more fun; but they fritter themselves away . . . Whenever anything is being accomplished, it is being done, I have learned, by a monomaniac with a mission. . . . The rest of us, with multiple interests instead of a single mission, are certain to fail and to have no impact at all. (*Adventures of a Bystander*, Peter F. Drucker, Harper Colophon Books.)

That's pretty hard on most of us. So let me tone it down with a qualification. I agree with Mr. Drucker, and I categorize myself with him; that is, I also am not a monomaniac. Being a monomaniac doesn't mean that a person can't have any other interests, but it does mean that he shouldn't do more than one thing at a time. This is an important difference. It boils down to this—success comes from concentrating one's energies. That energy can be targeted in only one direction at a time. If you want to move on to something else, burn the bridge and move on wholeheartedly.

I had another friend that had a similar experience but he could never make the break. Over the two years that I watched him, he made three times as much investing as he did in his business, but he couldn't zero in on either one. Consequently he floundered from one crisis to another—and neither one did very well.

An Expert on One Thing at a Time

The question, "Can a man serve two masters?" has timely importance here. There's a real tendency to think that if you're a real estate investor, you're an investor in every sense of the word. Take a few embarrassing pages out of my history: There were times when I would feel in control of the whole money market and I wanted to become a financial expert. I invested money in mutual funds and I even purchased some bonds. It would have taken five years to get the kind of return on them that I could have obtained in real estate in a few weeks, but I was going to be a financial expert. Now I realize that people spend years becoming experts in those areas. In my naiveté I assumed that because I was successful in one area I had a free ticket in all other areas. How wrong I was!

Becoming an expert in any field either requires a little effort over an extended time or an all out effort over a short time. But what is important is becoming the expert. To do this, you need to stick to one thing.

Diversify or Die

The pointed shaped building you see in San Francisco stands for diversification, and it's apparent how successful that company is. But we don't see all the companies that have failed because of too much diversification. There was a time when it was considered prudent to diversify—for tax purposes, growth, protection, etc. Now, a lot of those same companies are cutting back—ridding themselves of these other interests. Diversification causes new management problems and puts an excessive drain on the main company.

For us, individually, there is a time when we ask the same questions. "Should we diversify?" I answered, "yes" to that question, and it started me on a downhill slump.

I was heavy in to investing and because I wanted to be at the office more, I started a rental location service. It was draining my cash, but since the secretary was there, I also started another business. This one was a telephone answering service. I also reactivated my insurance agency to write insurance on all of my properties. These businesses started consuming my time. For six months I didn't buy one house. Then I took another step in the wrong direction. I started a major advertising business and sold several of my real estate contracts to support it. I wasn't able to give my all to any of these businesses that were crying for my attention. Finally, I realized the money for me was strictly in real estate. I had spent a long time developing these talents. With this realization I dissolved everything but the real estate. Hindsight is easy and if I could, I would change most of what I did during that time. Why quit doing that which is successful?

Don't Quit Doing That Which Is Successful

We all have tendencies to do this. I had a friend that sold thingamajigs. He would sell a modest amount until he would go to a convention somewhere like Bermuda. He'd come back all fired up and become the top salesman. After five or six months the high volume would stop and he'd be back to his old ways. Then he'd go to another convention in Hawaii and the process would be repeated. We talked about this one day and I asked him why this happened. He said he hadn't really noticed, but now that I mentioned it he wondered, too. Many people have answers for his behavior, but I said it seemed to me that his motivation came from the outside and not the inside. It's a lesson for all of us. When we're on track we should be like a horse with blinders on, and not quit while we're still in the race, or get sidetracked.

Ask the Right Questions

One of the most important things in becoming an expert investor is to ask the right questions. It's easy to put a lot of importance on having the right answers but too often they could be the right answers to the wrong questions. Both of my friends mentioned before were intelligent and had a strong desire to get ahead. I heard the questions that they asked themselves. The first friend, the one that couldn't make the break kept asking, "Does the money from investing help my business, and does the steadiness of my business help my investing?" The other friend asked, "In what area will I get the greatest return for my time and cash investment?" You can see by their answers which had the most effective question.

Don't stop because you might not have the right questions. In lieu of having the right questions, ask a LOT of questions. If you do this, eventually you will learn how to ask the right questions. When the right questions are asked, then the right information can be received in its proper light. It's like a giant computer—the answers are there, we just have to learn how to get at the information. Once this process becomes a way of life to the investor, the next step is to keep learning and keep adding current information to the stockpile. Usually, this opens up new questions, and it's this pursuit of excellence that makes for successful investing.

I'm reminded of a story about Albert Einstein sitting next to an eighteen year old girl at a big banquet. After a while she asked him what he did for a living. When he replied, "I'm engaged in the study of Physics," she responded, "Oh that. I studied that last semester!" Learning is an every day necessity in everything we do, especially in that which we desire to be successful.

Decision Making—Policy Making

These are the jobs of the executive—he needs to be a thinker. If he has properly surrounded himself with the right people and the right information then his task will be easier. He must realize that the decision making process starts with gathering opinions—hopefully conflicting opinions. Most of us gather facts to substantiate our beliefs. If you don't have contrasting opinions, you won't see all the sides. Don't make any decisions until you hear the adverse position. Build your decision on a foundation of contrasting opinions.

It's almost trite to say that there are two kinds of knowledge (that which you know and that which you have access to). No single person can know all there is about investing because there's too much to learn and it's constantly changing. Therefore, it behooves us to surround ourselves with a good team—people that are experts in their field and people that know how to ask the right questions and know where to look for the right answers.

The last thing an investor needs is "Yes" people in his life, because they will cause more harm than good. I found myself with people like this at times. Because there was so much going on—homes, rentals, contracts, repairs—they would be awed by it and nod their heads up and down at almost anything I wanted to do. I knew that I wasn't getting the proper negative feedback to help keep me on track. I wanted a challenge now and then to keep me thinking of alternatives. Luckily, I had a couple of friends that took everything I said with a questioning attitude. "Are you sure that's your only alternative?" "That doesn't seem like it follows your plan." "You're like a saw that never stops. You'd better get away from it and sharpen your blade." This is the kind of questioning I needed. I took those few friends to lunch often so I would have someone to throw a bucket of cold water on me when I needed it. Choose this team wisely—they could make or break you.

Make sure you have on your team:

1. One good real estate agent/broker.
2. A knowledgeable escrow and/or title officer.
3. A dependable real estate attorney (one who will be there when you need him).
4. A good tax consultant, and . . .
5. A good friend or two (another investor if possible).

Knowledge

There is no substitute for on-the-job training. Before I got into real estate investing I owned a small ice cream parlor. I didn't have a degree in business, or anything else that would help in this endeavor. I learned what I needed to know from DOING. Advertising, ordering, customer relations, hiring and firing, and all other skills I needed to be successful at that time came by asking the right questions to the right people; trying, making mistakes, and trying again. No formal education could have given me all I had learned, and I wouldn't trade those few years of experience for an MBA. The knowledge I gained has carried over into almost all other facets of my life.

I'm reminded of the story of a young reporter talking to a successful corporate executive.

"Why are you so successful?"

"Two words, son, two words, right decisions."

"And how did you learn to make right decisions?"

"One word, son, one word, experience."

"And how did you get experience?"

"Two words, son, two words, wrong decisions."

My hope is that you can see how this applies to real estate investing. If so, I'm confident that you are on the road to success.

Take Time Off

Another important question keeps surfacing: "When should an investor take time off?" That isn't an easy question to answer if your situation becomes like mine did.

The life you lead as an investor is an extremely exciting one. In fact, it is so exciting that you'll have trouble finding recreational activities that compare. Watching

TV will be boring, and you'll find yourself starting to fall asleep at the movies (unless it's a good Clint Eastwood movie). So my work became my hobby—I spent many hours thinking only of houses. It was all that I was interested in and it started to consume me. Before long, I was so wrapped up in the day to day details that I couldn't see the bigger picture. I couldn't make sure that I was continuing to operate in an effective manner—making sure that our cash could pay the bills and keep the program going. I started worrying about little things, instead of the whole concept. I had to force myself to take time out and get away from it—really get away.

I asked myself, "Does the corporate executive take time off?" "Yes," I thought. He goes golfing, and takes vacations. There was a period of time when I was so busy that I started making too many wrong decisions. Now when I look back, I realize how tired I was. I realized I had to get away from it. I was so tired I was getting sick of the pressures. It's like a child who plays all day then denies that he's tired. If the much needed rest doesn't come, one can't think straight. I do not claim to be an expert on the subject, but I know from experience that this kind of work requires constant brain power—it needs to be recharged now and then. There's no good time to leave this business. Just set your dates, take your spouse, and go. It will all be there when you get back. And remember you can take several two–three day trips instead of a long vacation. If you love this work, you'll love it even more if you can get away from it now and then.

There was a good movie out a few years ago called *Fiddler On The Roof*. The father in the film was constantly faced with answering questions that, for him, should have been easy, because he had tradition to guide him. But the questions needed new answers or at least a reevaluation of the old premises. At first, when confronted with these problems, he balked. Then the camera would zoom him off to the other side of the bridge or a field and he would carry on a conversation as if talking with God. He would come to a decision and then zoom back and solve the problem.

Wouldn't it be great if we could do all that? We can to some extent. I used to go for rides, or to the park—even if for a few hours. Be fresh and you won't get slapped.

The Over-Riding Concept of Success

Now that you are a monomaniac, becoming an expert, asking the right questions, setting up your team, learning every day, and taking the proper time off, we can tie it all into another concept—the over-riding concept that determines success or defeat. In order to do this, let's return to Peter Drucker for his comments on being effective. (I'll paraphase.) He states that the effective executive is one who has the ability to *get the right things done,* and *not* necessarily one that always *does things right.* (*The Effective Executive,* Peter F. Drucker, Harper & Row, Publishers.)

When I first understood this concept I was a little sad. I remembered all the times I had the emphasis turned around. How many costly delays were caused by my putting too much emphasis on doing things right? Now, don't think that I would scrimp on doing something the right way. Our motto in fixing something up was to do it as if we were moving in, but as the executive of my plan, I should have always been doing the right things. For example, I agree that employee relations are important and I always found time to converse with the people working with me, but one day I went to one of my houses that was having a roof put on. There were several guys up on the roof and after exchanging greetings one of them said, "Hey, grab a hammer and come up and listen to some good jokes." I love good jokes so it was hard for me to say, "If I do that, I won't be doing my work and you'll be out of a job."

Conclusion

Running around at a dizzying pace means nothing unless you're building and achieving. Keep things in perspective and build on the good talents you have as an individual—put your personality into it. The development of good executive attributes will pave the way for your success.

Chapter 18

Put the Machine on Automatic Pilot and Retire

NOW that you're flying high and want to reap the rewards of your investing, you must capitalize not only on the cash income you have created, but also on the talents and knowledge you have gained. The plan needs to have a built-in way for you to slow down but keep comfortably ahead. This method has an automatic pilot feature which can be turned on for continued income and growth.

Automatic pilot doesn't mean you can get out of the pilot's chair and sit back in first class for the rest of the trip. It means that you can use your time elsewhere as long as you stay near the controls.

If you think at some given age you will be able to turn your money over to someone else and have them perform with it the way you would, then you don't understand the nature of people. Your highest rates of return on your money will be made when you are there managing it. No matter how you invest your money, you need to keep control. The further you remove yourself from your money's control, the less you should expect to earn—and the less you will earn.

You have become successful because you invested your money in your own best interest. If you have invested successfully you will:

1. Have a rather large income
2. Have a real estate contract collection service to free you of this chore
3. Have an increasing equity growth, and
4. Have an understanding of contracts.

With this you can move on to another form of investing for which you have been trained.

In Chapter 5 we talked about the three important factors for someone who wants to buy contracts. These same factors hold true for you *now*.

They are:

1. Value of property
2. Yield on your money
3. Title status of the equity.

During the time of your investing you should have learned quite a bit about these three considerations. If you still don't fully comprehend them, don't despair, they will be explained in greater detail in this chapter.

You should take caution in trading your money for these longer term commitments. Let's review these three considerations and then point out a few more.

1. Make sure there is plenty of value above your loan. The lower the excess equity, the less you should be paying for a contract. For example: if you are buying the equity between a $50,000 receivable and a $40,000 payable and the house is worth $52,000 you are running a fine line. But if the value of that house is $70,000, then

there is plenty of protection as a buffer. In short, you want the people who are making payments to you to have a lot to lose, as an incentive for them to keep their payments current.

2. Yields—It's important to get your money back in as quickly as possible. Watch for high yields, but also remember:

   a. Buy contracts that will cash out as part of the agreement on a house qualifying for all types of financing later. (Typical investment properties have a higher probability of staying intact and not cashing out earlier than the final pay off date. Good residential property will sell many times.)

   b. Take a broad view of the whole equity structure. Sometimes properties with excellent equity protection might have a slightly lower yield.

   c. Watch your repay percent. Shoot for a one percent repay of the contract equity. If it's higher, great, but be cautious if it goes below that. You might be able to get it for a lower price, but in case you need to sell, it may be difficult.

3. Make sure you're buying what you bargained for—that your seller has no encumbrances against him, or that he hasn't encumbered his equity. You are buying his exact position so make sure you know what it is. Get title insurance.

4. Make sure you have the right to resell your contract. Buy contracts that others will also want to buy in case you have to sell to get at some cash.

5. If you don't like bookkeeping make sure you have an effective contract collection service handling your accounts.

6. Be on the lookout for good deals all the time. Let it be known through the paper or at real estate offices that

you're in the market. Be choosy. Take the ones that fit your needs.

7. Determine the location where you want your contracts to be. The opposing views are this:
   a. I want my contracts in several states in case one area is hit with hard times.
   b. I want them all right here in this city in case of problems.

I tend to agree with "b," as control is important.

8. Avoid contracts with all kinds of entanglements. This cannot be a gamble. Make sure there are definite time periods and some sort of penalties if the conditions of the contract are not met.

These are a few of the things to consider. There is so much that is subjective—factors that only you can put a value on. In a nut-shell, the price to pay is what you are willing to give.

In order to see what can be done for retirement, let's look at a set of contracts that would be a comfortable retirement for the average person. This represents two and a half years of work at two houses a month.

60 Contracts
×$11,000 Average Equity
$660,000 Total Equity

The following is the asset and liability breakdown:

$1,080,000 Assets
−420,000 Liabilities
$660,000 Total Net Worth

$105 Average monthly payment
×60 Contracts
$6,900 Total net monthly income

If you could live on $2,000 a month, what could you do with the excess $4,300?

Points to consider before answering that:

1. These payments come in for many years, but are not indefinite.

2. But long before they stop, the underlying loans are paid off, and your total net monthly income increases each time one pays off.

3. You are paying a relatively small amount of taxes each year on the installment method. You claim and deduct interest payments.

Now, you make the decision to slow down and start buying contracts. Then comes the exciting part. I've found that investing $4,000 to $5,000 a month in contracts takes about 3–5 hours a month. This time includes:

1. Placing an ad to buy contracts or other ways of notifying people of your intentions.
2. Negotiating the deal after you have:
   a. Obtained the title report.
   b. Looked at the property.
   c. Checked on other factors.
3. Closing the transaction.

Once you have tried this you will see how trouble free it is. Following the steps above you can take your $4,300 and buy a $7,500 contract or so with a $75 a month payment. Now let's see what you have done to your overall situation:

1. You still have the previous equity (and it's probably even a little larger now).

2. You have added to that equity a $7,500 contract.

3. You have added $75 a month to your income so next month you'll have $4,375 to do it again.

4. In terms of inflation, if your living requirements go up by 10 percent to $2,200 by the next year and you have purchased 12 contracts, you will have added around $900 (12 × $75) to your net monthly income. This is much more than the needed $200 increase and

because you will be purchasing increasingly larger contracts it will probably be even higher.

5. Some of these larger ones can be purchased by saving for a few months.

6. Taxes are handled on the installation sales method. For example: Let's say you buy a $10,000 contract for $6,000. Your profit will be $4,000. Divide that by the $10,000 and your installment profit ratio is 40 percent. Therefore, 40 percent of every principal payment needs to be claimed as you receive them. If the payment is $100, of which an average of $30 is principal—totaling $360 for the year—you will have to claim 40 percent of that or $144. (Remember interest income is treated as ordinary income).

7. You have added to your net worth and monthly payments another asset that is easy to handle and fully protected.

Consolidating Your Position

One of the most exciting aspects of reaching this point of having excess income is that you can now operate from a position of strength. Basically (if you want to keep moving forward—building your net worth and net monthly payments), there are two ways to go. One is to go out and find other people's contracts which we have already covered, but the second and probably the most logical is to buy the contracts which are your underlying payments. Notice that I didn't say pay them off, but buy them at a discount. From our previous example we ended up with $1,080,000 in assets and $420,000 in liabilities. These liabilities are made up of many people who would like to get at some cash. Wouldn't it be exciting if you could back that liability figure down to zero? Already the debt to asset ratio is excellent, but how much better would you feel if it were $320,000 or $220,000—and eventually zero?

Buying these underlying loans should be handled just like the others. Put out the word that you will pay people off, and eventually they will start selling—not always at first, but when they need cash they will know where to come. If someone has an $8,000 contract equity that you are making payments on, and they will take your $4,300 cash for it, how much better off would you be then? Many of the benefits are the same as the previous example, but a few are different.

1. You've changed your debt to asset ratio for the better.

2. You've eliminated one more payment, saving you time.

3. You may have gotten closer to the first position, and possibly have been able to assume their underlying loan at a lower interest rate.

In that you have 60 contracts, you probably have 80–90 underlying mortgages. You should look at them and make offers on the best ones. What is best in this case?

1. The ones with high interest rates.

2. The ones with higher payments in relationship to the mortgage amount.

3. The ones with excess restrictive clauses.

If you follow this course, within two years, you will have liabilities down to $220,000 and your net monthly payments will have grown from the $6,300 to $8,200.

Buy up all the inside contracts you can, but keep your eyes open for outside contracts also. You probably won't be able to purchase all of your payables at discounted rates. Some contracts won't be discounted. Banks seldom discount them to individuals even when it is in their best interests to do so. You should take an 8-cylinder approach to this concept.

Conclusion

All that I wanted in an investment plan came to fruition with this new approach. The *ease of this retirement aspect makes it all worthwhile.* You, also, will be able to enhance your position with very little effort. So put it on automatic pilot and *stay by the controls.*

Your money machine is intact and running smoothly. Now it's time to go fishing.

Appendix

Owner Financing

A Conversation with Wade B. Cook

The following question and answer conversation was carried on between myself and a skeptical radio personality not too long ago. I have included it at this point because it also answers many questions about the money machine concept that have been raised around the country. I am convinced you will find the information useful when you are dealing with people that want cash on their equity instead of monthly payments.

1. **Q. What exactly is meant by a contract or a contract sale?**

A. A contract for sale of real property is an agreement stipulating the conditions under which you will sell your property. Lately, it has taken on a general meaning of owner financing, meaning that the owner, instead of a bank, finances all or part of his equity.

The documents used could be a real estate contract or any of its cousins, a mortgage, or as is commonly becoming the norm, a deed of trust. But no matter which document is used, the gist is that the seller is carrying the financing, and he will earn the interest payments, not the bank.

2. Q. What other names may be found for transactions like that?

A. We might refer to it as a contract sale. It might also be called a wrap-around mortgage or an all-inclusive trust deed.

3. Q. Why did you sell on contract so many times?

A. Most of the properties that weren't sold on contract were in the first years of my investing. At that time I was continually faced with having to sell properties and when problems evolved from the tax consequences along with other problems from dealing with banks, I just naturally took the easier course, and what I consider to be the best course, which is to sell on contract.

To further answer your question, because I was willing to sell on contract, I was able to choose from a lot of different buyers who only had to live up to *my* standards and *my* qualifications, rather than the banks'. As I mentioned before, I was faced many times with selling my houses and I found that selling on contract was the easiest and fastest way to move them. I wanted to get some money back either on the down payments or on promises to receive money down the road, and to keep my investment plan turning.

I can empathize now with home sellers who are asking themselves the question as to whether or not they should sell on contract, because I was faced with that question so many times.

4. Q. Isn't the bookkeeping of selling on contract a big pain?

A. Not really. There are principal and interest payments coming in on the payments received. If it's a balloon payment, all you have to do is let the interest accrue and figure out what it's going to be at the end of the time. There are some questions concerning the taxes, yet, once the formula is understood, it's not that hard to compute. Let me explain further. When you're selling on contract, you'll be able to take advantages of claiming your profits as you receive them.

There is a simple ratio for figuring that out. All that is involved, basically, is taking the profit that you make on a piece of property, dividing it by the selling price, and coming up with a ratio. Now, you're going to apply that ratio to each and every principal payment as you receive them. That would include the down payment and any part of the monthly payments which goes to principal pay-off. Let me give an example. If you had a house that you bought for say, $30,000, and put $10,000 into fixing it up, and sold it for $50,000, your profit would be $10,000, which is the $50,000 minus the $40,000 cost basis. You would divide that $10,000 by the $50,000 and get .2 or 20%. 20% of all the principal payments that you receive, including the down payment and the monthly payments, would then be claimed as profit.

So instead of having to claim the entire $10,000 in the year that you sell the property, you are able to claim that $10,000 over the whole length of the contract, whether it be a 15, 20, or a 30 year contract. You'll be able to claim those profits *as you receive them*. Once that initial bookkeeping is done, another advantage comes through the ability to pay those taxes with inflated dollars.

5. Q. Do you have to claim it for tax purposes in that manner?

A. Not necessarily. Back to our example. If you want to claim the whole $10,000 this year, you may elect to do so. You do not have to claim on the installment sales method. Though I highly suggest that a person who is selling on installment sales would claim according to this method. Very few real estate properties are ever foreclosed on in proportion to the huge amount of properties that are bought and sold every day, but if a foreclosure ever did occur and you had already claimed the profits, you would have to back up and do a nice song and dance routine to get your money back.

If you claim the profits as you receive them and you foreclose, then you take the profits you have received so far, and end it there. Now you have the property back, which is probably worth more.

6. **Q. What about tax on the interest collected? Do I still have to claim that when selling on contract?**

A. Yes. If you have payments coming in, you will have to claim the interest as ordinary income. *That's the beautiful cost of making a profit.*

7. **Q. Is there any limit as to how many properties I can sell on contract at one time?**

A. No. Not only is there no limit to how many different properties you can buy and sell on contract, but also there is no limit to how many times the same piece of property can be bought and sold on contract. For instance, you might buy it from somebody on contract, turn around and sell it a year later to somebody else on contract. You might have A paying B, B paying C, C paying D, and so on.

8. **Q. Does the contract itself have any value other than just collecting money every month? Can it generate any other kind of income?**

A. Yes. Let's go back to our example. Let's say, for instance, that we wanted to avoid taxes, and we see on installment sales and are able to take our $10,000 and spread it out over the whole length of the time we receive it. Also, let's say that we take nothing for a down payment and we just have a $10,000 contract with $100 a month coming in. Now our situation changes all of a sudden. We do need a little bit of cash. We can take that equity contract down to the bank, use it as collateral for a loan and because we're getting a loan, which is borrowed money, *we pay no taxes on that money.*

So our contract can be used effectively for collateral purposes. Be sure, though, to keep the ownership of the contract in your name. If it is going to be pledged as security, it should state so. It should say, "the assignment of this contract is given for collateral purposes only." Also, if you're getting a loan from the bank and the bank wants to receive the payments from the contract, have the money deposited into your savings account and then drawn out to make the loan payment.

Whatever you do, make sure that all the wording stays in your name and there is no real assignment to the bank. If there is an assignment to the bank, the IRS might deem it a sale and make you claim your profits at that time.

9. Q. What about other tax laws that apply to selling on contract? Do I still qualify for a long-term capital gain?

A. Yes. If you hold a property for over one year, you will be obligated to claim only 40% of the amount that you receive. Let's go back to our example. Let's change it a little bit this time, though, and say that we received a $2,000 down payment. Of the $2,000 down payment we're only going to have to claim 20% of that, which is our installment sales ratio. So we'll only have to claim $400 this year (20% × $2,000). If we had held this property for over a year before we sold it, we would only have to claim 40% of the $400, or $160.

10. Q. Should all properties be held for one year so you can take advantage of this situation?

A. No, not necessarily. If the person's long-term goal is to hold property for a year in order to be able to sell it and take advantage of long-term gain, that's fine. I would say, traditionally, that would be a very applicable way of deferring taxes or avoiding taxes, if the person is buying the property and holding it for the appreciation in value and for the other tax write-offs.

If, however, a person is trying to capitalize on turning a piece of property and he thinks that he can make a fair profit, the installment sales ratio (being able to claim profits as received) is a great enough tax incentive to sell a piece of property. Let me give you an example. Suppose a property has a high negative cash flow, meaning that a person has a property and the rents coming in are less than the payments going out. If he can turn that same piece of property by selling it and receive higher monthly payments from somebody else buying it from him, then many times it would be in his best interest to sell the property, to alleviate the negative cash flow which can be a real burden to people, and to get some kind of a down payment or some kind of monthly payments coming in so that he can take the money and reinvest it in still other properties.

It does not even have to have a negative cash flow. Some people may be tired of rental headaches and would rather have a steady monthly income, letting *someone else* worry about collecting rents. Other times, people may be moving and can't worry about the problems. A nice check in the mailbox once a month is no worry at all.

11. Q. What kind of equity contracts are there?

A. An equity contract refers to the amount of

money that is now owing the seller or lienholder. For instance, in our previous example, where the owner sold the property for $50,000, he has two options for creating an equity contract. He can either let somebody else assume his existing loans and pay him his equity on contract, or he may carry the whole balance of the loan and receive monthly payments on the whole amount. This method leaves the underlying loans intact. The seller stays responsible for them and makes the payments on these underlying loans.

12. Q. What are some of the advantages of each way? Obviously, a person can do either.

A. Okay, let's talk about the first one, where the seller lets the buyer assume his loans. The advantage of this way is that he no longer is responsible for making the monthly payments on the existing loans or liens. This can be quite a hassle for some people. All the seller is going to do is receive monthly payments. For example, let's assume his equity is $20,000. He and the buyer agree on $200 a month. He will have that amount to spend with no other obligations. The advantages of the second way are two-fold. The seller is going to maintain a little bit more control. Now, he's going to have to ask himself if this control is worth it. He is going to keep the underlying loan. He knows the underlying payment is going to be made because he is the one making it. The buyer is going to give him say, a $500 a month payment, and he will be making a $300 a month payment on the underlying loan (if those are the payments).

He then will have his $200, but it will represent the difference between the $500 payment and the $300 payment. The other point in this: When he sells on a wraparound contract, he is not only going to be earning interest on the $20,000. He'll be earning interest on the unpaid balance of the $50,000 loan. Let's say the underlying interest rate is 10%. He will only get a 2% spread on the $30,000. But he will be getting the full interest on the $50,000 loan. So there is a difference in interest amounts.

13. Q. Let's say I have a house, I've sold it on contract, I have some people making payments for three years, and all of a sudden—no payments. The people disappear. What do I do? What are my options?

A. Both the buyer and the seller are protected under the terms of the contract. If the buyer does not make the payments, or does not live up to the obligations of the contract, it would just be an easy foreclosure, to divest the buyer of his rights to the property. If they've disappeared and they're not making the payments anymore, it is a simple process to get the property back. Now you would have the property back and would be able to sell it at hopefully a higher price, because of inflation. One might think that the buyer might run down the house. But in all of my contracts it was very seldom the case. Usually the buyer, because he's buying and is not just renting, comes in and fixes up the house. I've only had one bad experience where the buyer was starting to fix up the house; he had in fact ripped out several walls in a major attempt to remodel and made the house less attractive than it was before. He died and left the house in a bad state. His wife couldn't fix it up and I ended up getting the house back in worse condition than it was in when I sold it.

But in over 30 houses on contract, the buyers improved the houses by putting on additions; fixed up the interior and exteriors, and took care of the yards. But if you do need to enforce your rights, it's a simple matter of contacting an attorney and starting the process. This legal expense will have to be paid by your buyer before they can reinstate the loan with you. Your rights are very strongly worded in the real estate contract or deed of trust.

If you foreclose on a seller, you will need to work with a very good attorney so that you can understand the state laws in regards to the buyer's rights; namely, whether you need to return any money to him or refund any equity that he has built up. Basically, in most states, when you foreclose, you get the house back *"as is, where is."* The house becomes yours once again. You are free to sell it or dispose of it in any way you please. If you sold a house for $50,000 and you had to foreclose on the person, and the house is now worth $60,000 in value, you have an asset of $60,000 that you can turn around and sell again and have a bigger monthly payment coming in or whatever.

But the main point is that the provisions of the contract literally protect you.

14. Q. Is there anything in particular that I can do at the onset of the contract that will help insure that the payments will keep coming in?

A. Well, the payments are basically stated in the contract. There's nothing more that you would want to add to that. The wording is there and it is worded in the seller's favor. If there are other terms that you are agreeing to, yes, you would want to make sure that they are in precise language, stated right in the contract that both of you sign. This will make sure that there is *no misunderstanding of the obligations that both of you need to perform.*

15. Q. What about insurance? Someone's buying my house on contract. Do I maintain insurance or is that their obligation?

A. That is their obligation. Likewise, it will state in one of the paragraphs of the real estate contract that the buyer will get insurance, at least enough to cover the loan balance owing you, but usually he'll get insurance to cover the fair market value of the house. You don't need to carry insurance.

You would be listed as the loss payee, or the policy will have a contract of sale document. You and any other people who have a lien against the property would also be listed on the insurance policy. Now, if the buyer ever lapses his policy or *even gets close* to having the policy lapse, you will also receive notice and will be able to take precautions at that time to protect yourself.

16. Q. What have you found are the best methods for advertising properties for sale?

A. When an owner is willing to sell a house on contract and is willing to do so with very flexible terms, meaning that he is able to take a low down payment or no down payment and carry the contract, the best way to get to the largest number of buyers so he can pick and choose from among the best, is to advertise through the newspaper.

I also know that I enjoy selling my properties to other investors. I know that investors are coming in to use the properties as rental units or possibly to fix them up further and re-sell them. I know they're looking for a place to make improvements, not just a place to hang their hat; they want a place to improve, to build some equity of their own. For this reason, *I even look for investors.* I know several of them and go to them and say, "I've got a number of properties for sale. Let's see if we can work out a deal."

17. Q. I've heard of people selling their contracts. Is that a possibility?

A. Yes. There are a lot of people out there who think very highly of real estate contracts. What are you going to get for your contract? Obviously, if these investors are going to be taking their money down the road and they're going to be giving you cash today, they want to give you a discounted amount.

Now, I know a lot of people who do just that. They *buy a property, fix it up,* and *sell it* on contract, because they can sell it so quickly, and then they turn right around, discount the contract and sell it. I would suggest, as stated earlier, if you need cash, one of the first things you should do is get a loan using your contract as collateral, because you'll pay no taxes.

If you in fact do sell the contract, you're going to have to pay taxes. You'll have an adjusted basis now. Let's use our example again. If your cost basis is $40,000 and you sell it for $50,000, you will have a $10,000 equity contract which could sell for $6,000 cash. What you're really saying is that you really didn't sell the house for $50,000, you sold it for $46,000. Okay, now you just have to refigure that and submit it on your tax forms. Now that you have this cash you have to claim it in the year you sell the contract. If you're looking for sources of selling contracts, they're usually in the paper. There are usually a lot of people looking to buy contracts. Look under *Real Estate Contracts for Sale* or possibly under *Money to Loan.*

What they are willing to pay for it all depends on what they consider important. Some people look at the interest rates you are charging. Some people look at the monthly payments or any balloon payments to see how fast their money will come back in. Some of them will look at the costly position of the contract. If it's at the top end, or the middle, they put different values on it.

When it comes right down to it, what you're going to get for your contract is what somebody is willing to pay for it. But you can enhance that amount by shopping. If I had a contract for sale, and I've sold a lot of my contracts, I would just call four or five people and say,

"Here are the figures. Here's the address. What would you give me for this?" And then I just take the highest bidder.

18. Q. What about balloon payments?

A. If you need cash at some future time and it is agreeable to the buyer, then maybe some kind of arrangement for larger-than-normal payments, due at some future date, may be in line. But I don't like them.

Once in a while I agreed to them when I was purchasing property, but in every case they turned out to be real headaches. I told myself that I would never make anybody promise to pay me one, and I got along splendidly without them. There are too many things that can get out of control which can place real hardships on people. I just wanted the steady monthly payments.

19. Q. What interest rates should I charge if selling on contract? Should I charge what the banks are charging?

A. Let's look at the main housing problem that exists in America today. Because of high interest rates, smaller banks are forced to pay such high amounts for their money that they must loan out their money at even higher rates. These interest rates disqualify buyers—they can't afford the high monthly payments. It used to be that if you bought a house for $50,000, the payments were going to be between $450–$500. Now if you buy a house for $50,000, the payments are going to be between $650–$700.

Not many people who want to live in a house of this size can even qualify for the loan. So what the banks have done is price themselves right out of the market. I know savings and loans and banks all over the country right now that are not even making loans. They tell their customers that they don't feel justified in charging higher rates, and maybe that's true, but they don't *have* the money to loan at these high rates and they're having such a hard time qualifying people. I talked to one loan officer who said that he had talked to 15 people for an average sized house and only one qualified. So they shut down their loan officer's desk, realizing they were just wasting their time.

Now, if you as a seller want to find yourself in the same position of not having any buyers who can afford the house or make the payments, then go ahead and charge the high interest rates. But if, in fact, you would like somebody to come in and buy your property, and you're more concerned about having a nice, steady monthly income, then I would suggest that you charge a rate that is fair. Fair is what you and the buyer can negotiate; what is affordable.

I think it is fair to charge what banks are paying on their loans, not what they're charging. For instance, if the banks are paying 10–11% for a savings account and they're charging 17% on their loans, then maybe you ought to look at charging 10–11%. Then you'll have people who can afford to buy a property, and you'll have a lot of buyers to choose from.

20. Q. Once we're ready to sign the papers, is there someone who can help me, the novice, fill out the papers so it's all legal?

A. Yes. Obviously, attorneys are very adept at filling out the forms. Title companies and escrow companies can also fill out the forms. Forms are drawn up, though, in such a simple manner, that it's almost a fill-in-the-blank process. There are books written that literally give the terminology and phraseology that can be used for filling in the details.

I suggest the easiest place to go is to a good escrow officer who can process all of the papers. If he can't handle the entire transaction, he can bring in other competent help. You can share with them your fears, the things that you want, and the things negotiated between you and the buyer and the escrow person will include these things in the right places.

21. Q. What are the steps I need to follow to sell my property this way?

A. The following steps are given as a basic guideline. Different properties may require additional footwork, but generally speaking, selling your property will come together properly if you:

Step 1. Do some research on the value of your property. Also determine what you're willing to take and how you're willing to take it.

Step 2. Sit down with your buyer and negotiate the exact terms. Make suggestions and be open to suggestions. Compromise when necessary. Remember, one-sided deals may fall flat. Make sure everyone benefits.

Step 3. Draw up an earnest money agreement. Don't trust anything to just the spoken word. This agreement will become the foundation for the whole transaction, so fill it out in detail.

Step 4. Deliver the earnest money agreement and any changes or addendums to an escrow company (or whomever you choose to handle the closing) and have them start drawing up the papers.

Step. 5. Go about doing anything that you are committed to doing while your buyer does the same.

Step 6. Inspect the papers carefully. Don't assume anything. Make sure they are exactly what you want.

Step 7. Sign the papers and transfer possession of the property.

22. Q. Let's say I choose to sell on contract. Can I do it with a Realtor? And if so, does it demand that I ask a bigger down payment?

A. The answer is yes and no. Yes, you may sell your house on contract with a Realtor acting as your agent. In many cases if both the seller and the buyer know absolutely nothing about real estate using a Realtor would be appropriate.

A good real estate agent fills a vital roll for people who do not understand real estate. The good ones are worth every dollar they earn. Because of the stagnant lending situation, many of them are becoming the champions of creative and flexible financing. Their innovative solutions have glued together many deals that may have been discarded. Sit with them and explain your needs. Let them come up with the solutions.

Whether or not you have to charge a larger down depends on the relationship with the real estate company. If the company is willing to take their commissions on contract with monthly payments, or is willing to take their commissions on a note payable at some future time, you would not have to charge more cash as a down payment.

If the real estate company absolutely demands cash, then the seller has two choices. He can either pay the real estate company the cash and therefore have to demand more down from his buyer or he can find another real estate company that is willing to be more flexible with their commissions.

23. Q. In all actuality, do real estate agents ever really take their commissions on contract?

A. Yes. And the more troubled this real estate market gets, with these high interest rates, and the fewer number of sales that are made, the more flexible they become. Remember though, they need to eat, too. Look around for a good agent. What they're saying now is, "Hey, I might as well have this money payable at 12% interest a year from now, or whatever, than nothing." So they're able to squeeze these deals into their normal activities.

24. Q. When selling a house on contract, what about other costs I have incurred? For instance, property taxes and insurance that I have already paid in advance?

A. There will actually be a day where the title to the property will transfer and the documents will be recorded. This is the closing date. All of these costs that you mentioned, and other costs, will be pro-rated to this day. For instance, let's say that you made the insurance payment for the month and the date of closing is in the middle of the month. The payment that you have already made will have to be paid to you by the buyer from the day of closing.

If property taxes have been paid for the whole year and you're closing the property on July 1, then there will be a refund to you of half of the property taxes that you have already paid. Everything will be pro-rated. By the way, that's exactly what escrow companies are good at: figuring out to the day who has what coming to them so that there is no discrepancy.

25. Q. Who are the people who should sell their house on contract?

A. Why don't we reverse the question and ask who is not going to want to sell their house on contract? We'll answer that first. If a person has already committed money to buy another piece of property, he is going to be very desperate in that he needs some cash out of the property he's selling to buy into something else. Those people are not going to be very flexible. They might have to be flexible on their price just to get at the cash. For instance, they might have to sell a $90,000 home for $80,000 just to come up with the cash they need.

But if a person can control how much money he's going to need for the future property and keep that amount very low, he'll be able to sell this present house and receive less money, allowing him to take his equity on contract with payments coming in.

Now to answer your question. I have seen rich people, I have seen poor people, I have seen young and old sell their houses on contract. I've negotiated deals with people from all walks of life and that's not what's important. Their current status only effects them in terms of how they view their options. A person would have to figure out what they want for themselves—whether they want the monthly payments coming in, whether they want cash, or whether they are willing to take a lower price for the house to get at cash. It's just a matter of sitting down with the people and seeing what they want.

26. Q. Obviously, there are advantages to both the cash-out and in getting monthly payments. How does a person know which way to go?

A. He needs to ask himself, "What is cashing-out going to do to my tax situations? Do I need the cash? What am I going to do with it? Can I get a high return if I finance this buyer?" Let me tell you a few other things. It's been my experience that when people get cash, somehow all of a sudden it seems to disappear. One time I saw a couple get $10,000 out of their house and in just a few months the money was gone. Their plans for investing it, sticking it into this and that went up in smoke in a few short months, they had nothing to show for it.

I had another friend who sold a house for a $15,000 equity contract with $200 a month coming in. Every month that money would come in like clockwork. They loved it. Their rationale was that it was grocery money. The monthly bills keep coming in and it's nice to have those payments coming in to meet them.

One other thing—and this is more of an intrinsic value to having a steady monthly income coming in. You know, as you look at gold, silver, and the stock market right now, you see huge ups and downs. You see the constant fluctuating even more so when a president is shot, or with interest rates going up a couple of points, etc. Let's be quite honest; there have been a few dips in the real estate market in the past century, but the dips have been very mild, and all in all, over the last 1,000 years the price of real estate has continued to go up with very few set-backs or recessions affecting it.

You're talking about one property that is comparable to another property on a daily basis. This house in this neighborhood sold for this much so this other house will sell for this much. Because of that, there is a great stability that is added and it enhances the real estate market.

I know a lot of people who feel better about their lives, about themselves, because they have a steady monthly income coming in on these contracts. Not only retired people, but all kinds of people who know that they have $200, $500 and even $1,000 a month coming in on their contracts secured by real estate. They know that this money is going to be there month after month.

27. Q. With your books, your lecturing and your experience, you have a pretty good feel for buying and selling on contract. Let me ask this: Is owner financing just a thing of today or will it be around for awhile?

A. Let's not answer that in terms of looking at the present and then predicting the future. Let's answer it in terms of the past. Owner financing existed long before bank financing. For years, people have been selling property and receiving payments or some kind of trade item for their property.

Along comes the government and along comes heavy

bank financing. The banks can loan money and be protected with FNMA, FHA and VA loans. The whole emphasis in the market for the last 50 years has changed to bank financing. The banks came to control the whole market. They were controlling interest rates. They were controlling who qualified, etc. Now all of a sudden, banks are finding that they are out of control because people can't live up to their standards.

But people haven't changed their minds. They're just looking for other ways to buy a house. Looking down the road, all I can say is that if the interest rates stay high then there's going to be a big demand for owner financing. I think this is creating a new awareness in all of the real estate industry as it deals with real estate agents, brokers, investors, and the average home buyer and seller. They're realizing that bank financing is not the only way.

There are other sources of money. There is a necessity out there for people to keep buying and selling houses. If they can't do it one way, they'll back up, take another look, and do it another way. And once the mind is expanded, it never goes back to its original dimension. The American people will continue to develop more and better solutions.

28. Q. So you're saying that if the interest rates go down it will have little effect on owner financing?

A. Yes. We will still see owner financing, but it will have effects in other ways. Let's give a hypothetical case. I sold a house for $70,000 and charged 14% interest with a monthly payment of $800 per month, my equity in the property being $20,000. If the interest rates dropped down to about 8 or 9%, and the person buying the house would realize that he could refinance his $70,000 loan to me and owe $70,000 to somebody else and have a monthly payment of $500 or $600 a month he will then refinance it and I'm going to receive my $20,000 as a pay-off.

Somebody else will stand in my place now and I won't have anything else to do with the property. Let's carry that one step further. One of the things that I liked to do was to sell my house on contract, because I could get that money working again on other houses. I learned at that time that the average American lives in his house for 3 to 5 years and then sells it.

Most people still believe that bank financing is the only way, so they're out selling their houses with some sort of bank financing. I would get cashed out. I was told that the average time was 3 to 5 years, but with my houses it happened on an average of every two years. So even though I sold on contract, at some time down the road I got cashed out of all the money that was owed to me.

29. Q. So in other words, selling on contract now with high interest rates is not going to hurt me in the long-run even if interest rates go down, except in the sense of having the security of payments?

A. Yes, that's true. You need to understand that there is a chance that once you sell your house on contract, the contract may run for the whole 20, 25, or 30 years. It happens very seldom but could happen. If the rates come down, there's a chance that the person will sell or refinance the house. The only thing that I have learned in my years of investing that always holds true is that nothing remains constant; everything changes. The circumstances will change and the seller will more than likely be on to other things in a few years.

30. Q. Are there other advantages to selling on contract?

A. We constantly hear about the amount of

money that a house will cost by the time it's paid for. For example, a $50,000 house will cost over $150,000 by the end of 25 or 30 years. If we reverse this idea and realize that if we sell in this way, that this additional money will be ours.

Let's say that we have $20,000 equity in a property and receive it on a note at $200. We really need the cash but by doing it this way in 6 or 7 years we will have received our $20,000 and our buyer will still owe us about $19,000 (the major part of the payment is interest, with very little going to principal pay off). Carrying it further—in another 6 or 7 years we will have received another $20,000 and he'll still owe us about $13,000.

It's great to get all of this money instead of the banks.

31. Q. As a short summary then, why should I sell on contract?

A. Well, the first thing is the fact that it might be your only way of selling. Nobody may be able to qualify for your house at the price you're asking. You're going to find a lot of buyers. You're going to have a nice monthly payment coming in. You're going to be able to pay taxes on your profit as you receive it. The amount owed to you is going to be fully protected and secured by real estate. The amount is going to be under the actual value of the real estate and as the value continues to increase, the value position of your loan is going to be strengthened. So, all in all, you are protected. Your investment is strong and healthy.

We think that it is important to understand all the formulas for selling your house creatively, but it is even more important for you to understand exactly how all of these formulas and ratios apply to your specific property. Therefore, please use the easy-to-fill-out form below to see exactly what your property will yield you in terms of your installment sales computation, cash to

CALCULATIONS FOR YOUR PROPERTY

1st year

1. Selling Price $________
2. Purchase Cost $________
3. Improvement Costs $________
4. Other Costs $________
5. Total Costs (Basis) (Add lines 2 thru 4) $________
6. Profit from Sale (Subtract line 5 from line 1) $________
7. Installment Sales Ratio
   Line 6 ÷ Line 1 (Profit Sales Price) = _____% or _____
8. Down Payment Received $________
9. Estimated Monthly Payments to be received (Principal Only) $________
10. Total (Lines 8 & 9) $________
11. Total (Line 10) _________ × _________ (Ratio from line 7) = _________ THIS IS THE AMOUNT TO CLAIM IF PROPERTY IS HELD FOR LESS THAN ONE YEAR.

Note: If your property is held for over 365 days, your gain will qualify as a long term capital gain and only 40% of the amount received needs to be claimed.

2nd year

12. Estimated principal payments to be received in the second year $_________
13. Amount from line 12 _________ × Ratio (Line 7) = CLAIMED IN THE SECOND YEAR. If long term, then multiply this figure by current long term rate.

3rd year, 4th year, etc.—The same calculation carries on from year to year. IRS form 6252 is used for reporting property sold on the installment sales method.

you, monthly payments or balloon payments. We realize that the tax consequences of selling property is one of the largest considerations and therefore the form on this page is designed to answer that problem.

Publisher's Note

The preceding conversation is published in a 20 page brochure by ITP and sells for $2.00. The reason we have published this in brochure form is for you to use as a handout to people to help them understand the beauty of taking monthly payments instead of their equity in cash. Just think how nice it would be to have people refuse to take cash because of the advantages of taking monthly payments as presented here in this chapter and in the brochure. For ordering *Owner Financing,* see the suggested reading list in the back of the book.

The following books have been reviewed by the staff of ITP and suggested as reading and resource material for your continuing education to help you with your real estate investment. Because new ideas and techniques come along and laws change, we're always updating our catalog. If you would like an updated catalog, write to:

ITP, Inc.
P.O. Box 1201
Orem, Utah 84057
or call (801) 224-3500.

Recommended List of Real Estate Seminars

AS I've traveled the country the past few years I've had the privilege of meeting several individuals teaching seminars on various aspects of real estate. There are so many bad ones that it was a pleasure to meet the instructors and attend the seminars listed below. Please write or call them to get their schedules.

1. The Real Estate Money Machine Seminar. Since this is mine let me list it first. My company has worked hard to put on seminars with solid functional information. Seminars are taught on several aspects all over the country. I personally sponsor whole conventions and teach 8 different sessions in one to two day formats. We have all day Saturday lectures all over the country. For a speaking schedule please write ITP, P.O. Box 1201-M, Orem, UT 84057 or call 801-224-3500.

2. Nothing Down. Bob Allen set the investment world on fire a few years ago with his ideas. His book and seminars are renowned all over the country. He keeps current with books and a newsletter and has his ideas taught extensively through a seminar out of Reno,

NV. For information on his books, tapes, or newsletter write The Allen Group, 145 E. Center Dept BW, Provo, UT 84601.

3. Prosperity Workshops. Phil Drummond is one of the most talented and knowledgeable authors and lecturers on the circuit. He's out of Florida and travels widely teaching at his exciting seminars. This is a great seminar for the beginner and anyone with little money and a lot of energy. Write him at 515 Adanson Street, Dept DC, Orlando, FL 32804.

4. Joe Land Seminars. Rarely does one individual perfect an angle of real estate investing as Joe Land has done with buying property with paper. (Mortgage agreements, Deeds of Trust, Bonds, etc.) A premier lecturer and down to earth educator—you'll really get excited about what he has to teach. Send for his free 45 minute tape that explains his concepts. Write to Joe Land, P.O. Box 11156 Dept LW, Albuquerque, NM 87192-00156.

5. National Institute of Financial Planning. Mark Haroldson has done so much to help people from all walks of life get started and make big money in real estate. He and his company are dynamos in the education field. It's great to find people so willing to share what they know. NIFP sponsors seminars and conventions nationwide. Write NIFP, 1831 Ft. Union Blvd. Dept MW, Salt Lake City, UT 84111.

6. Hal Morris. This man is great. He teaches some of the best techniques anywhere. His lectures and seminars appeal to beginners and experienced alike. He gets specific with foreclosures, and using other investor's money to make millions. I recommend his courses highly. Write him at 175 S. Los Robles Ave. Dept MC, Pasadena, CA 91101.

7. Steve Thomas. This broker, investor, counselor

has so many great ideas he can't get them all in to his seminar. He packs rooms across the country with people learning his "Zero Down" concepts. His techniques work. He travels and teaches in all states on an exhaustive speaking schedule. Write him at 101 E. 2000 S. Dept. TC, Orem, UT 84057 or call 801-226-0364.

8. Wayne Phillips. Finally a seminar is out that lets people tap the huge resources the government throws out for investors. Nobody knows this area of investment like Wayne does. You won't be disappointed a bit with his books, tapes and seminars. As a matter of fact, you'll be thrilled. Write him at 4 E. Biddle St. Dept WW, Baltimore, MD 21202 or call 301-528-1600.

9. David Shamy Seminars. David is one of the most vivacious authors and lecturers in the country. His approach to landlording and building cash flows stand as a hallmark to competent, professional approaches by making your small investments work for you in big ways. I can't say enough good about his seminar. Write him at P.O. Box 9301 Dept. SW, Salt Lake City, UT 84109.

10. Jimmy Napier. This "down home country boy" knows his business. He is uniquely qualified to write and lecture. If only I'd have heard him 5 years ago what a difference it would have made. Every one will learn tons of information from his lectures. Small town boys do make it big. You need to hear him. Write: P.O. Drawer F Dept. JC, Chipley, FL 32428.

11. Paul Cook. Paul coauthored a book with me entitled *Big Bucks by Selling Your Property*. His approach to making money in real estate is really exciting. Every piece of information is solid and functional. He is traveling the states teaching his concepts and helping a lot of people out of some of the messes they've found themselves in because of investing with antiquated methods.

You'll get a kick out of what he has to say. Write: P.O. Box 1031 Dept. CC, Orem, UT 84057.

12. Tracy Sandberg Real Estate Seminar. Tracy has authored several books on real estate including, *How To Lose Your Shirt in Real Estate: 26 Common Mistakes to Avoid, The Great Mortgage Money Mystery* and *Here We Go Round the Due on Sale Clause.* He teaches the A to Z's of structuring deals in an exciting way. He can be reached at 21 E. Howell Ave. Dept TW, Alexandria, VA 22301.

13. Greg James. It's exciting to see someone so knowledgeable teaching what he knows. Greg is a syndication expert. Partnerships can be great if done properly. He'll teach you how to take all the great ideas you learn and put them to work in big ways. His seminar is so good because it is so practical. His books are excellent. Write: Greg James, 5322 E. Nees Ave. Dept GC, Clovis, CA 93612.

Obviously the list could go on. ITP sponsors and co-sponsors seminars from coast to coast. These other seminars are listed in the Money Machine monthly newsletter. Education unlocks the door of tomorrow. I don't regret one penny spent on my education. I don't think you will either. As a matter of fact, I can't think of any area of investment that will make you more money than investing in your own gray matter.

Suggested Reading Material

HOW TO BUILD A REAL ESTATE MONEY MACHINE—TAPE
by Wade B. Cook
A 2-hour seminar by Wade Cook on what is fast becoming the most popular method in the country for investing in real estate **$29.95**

HOW TO BUY REAL ESTATE TAX BENEFITS—BOOK
by Wade B. Cook
At last! You can get an "easy to understand" book on how to use the tax laws to your advantage when you invest in real estate. In just one year this book has saved thousands of dollars for people all over the country **$24.95**

THINGS YOUR CPA NEVER TOLD YOU—TAPE
by Wade B. Cook
A 2-hour seminar on the subject of real estate and taxes. Easy to understand and very easy on your pocketbook when tax time rolls around **$29.95**

COOK'S BOOK ON CREATIVE REAL ESTATE
Fine Tuning the Money Machine by Wade B. Cook
This book will teach you all the "ins and outs" of

putting together creative real estate deals. It will even show you how to get your real estate agent to help you! This is a popular book on the lecture circuit **$24.95**

BIG BUCKS BY SELLING YOUR PROPERTY
by Paul D. Cook and Wade B. Cook

You've probably seen and read dozens of books that tell you how to buy real estate, but finally here's a book that explains the art of making big money by selling property—Don't miss this one! **$14.95**

HOW TO PICK UP FORECLOSURES
by Wade B. Cook

A poor economy has left thousands of opportunities in the real estate market for the investor to turn some big profits quickly. This book teaches how to deal with the most lucrative area of real estate investing from beginning to end **$24.95**

OWNER FINANCING
by Wade B. Cook

A 20 page pamphlet you can give to buyers who hesitate to sell you their property using the owner financing method. Let this pamphlet convince them for you **$2.50**

RECORD KEEPING SYSTEM
by Wade B. Cook

A complete record system for keeping all information on your properties organized. Keeps track of everything from insurance policies to equity growth. Know exactly where you stand with your investment properties and sleep at night **$17.95**

LEGAL FORMS

60 legal forms used in real estate transactions are included. This booklet is bound so the forms may be eas-

ily duplicated on a copy machine. The forms were selected by experienced investors, but are not intended to replace the advice of an attorney **$17.95**

THE THREE ENTITY APPROACH TO INVESTING IN REAL ESTATE
by Wade B. Cook

A method of using yourself, your corporation, and your pension and profit sharing plan for investing in real estate. Triple your effectiveness as an investor. (Includes a prototype for a pension and profit sharing plan.) **$17.95**

THE FIRST NATIONAL BANK OF REAL ESTATE CLAUSES
by Wade B. Cook

Every investor has been waiting for this book. Now a reference book filled with over a thousand clauses for putting your investment deals together is finally made available to the public and better yet, it's easy to understand. (Available after April 22, 1983) **$34.95**

A DAY WITH WADE COOK—TAPES

SPEND 8 "jam-packed" hours of real estate education with one of the foremost experts in the country today. You'll experience a thorough, easy to understand seminar that can lead you to financial independence, wherever and whenever you're in the mood to listen. (Available after April 15, 1983) **$125.00**

RED HOT REAL ESTATE IDEAS—TAPES

34 hours of real estate education conveying about every topic in real estate you can imagine. You'll receive instruction from over a dozen nationally prominent real estate experts who specialize in what they'll be teaching you. No one should miss this one! **$154.95**

CONTROL WITHOUT OWNERSHIP
by Phil Drummond

Package includes 3 ring binder with workbook materials and 6 hours of tapes covering over 50 proven methods to make money in real estate without having to own a single property **$99.95**

REAL INVESTORS DON'T FEED ALLIGATORS
by Phil Drummond

A humorous view on how to avoid negative cash flows. A poignant approach to increasing income and lowering expenses. You'll love it! **$9.95**

HOW TO LOSE YOUR SHIRT IN REAL ESTATE
by Tracy Sandberg

Mr. Sandberg covers 26 mistakes you should **avoid** to keep from "losing your shirt" as a real estate investor **$9.95**

THE GREAT MORTGAGE MONEY MYSTERY
by Tracy Sandberg

This book will help you understand the many different types of loans available today and how to use each of them to your advantage **$9.95**

THE GREAT MORTGAGE MONEY MYSTERY—TAPE
by Tracy Sandberg

Spend 2 hours in the privacy of your home learning how you can use the money lenders to your advantage as a real estate investor. Great resource material to refer back to time and time again **$24.95**

HERE WE GO 'ROUND THE DUE ON SALE' CLAUSE
by Tracy Sandberg

Learn how to fight back when confronted with the

infamous 'due on sale' clause. Don't let it limit your investment opportunities **$19.95**

THE SMART INVESTOR'S GUIDE
by Robert Bruss

Nationally prominent investment columnist, Robert Bruss shares his expertise on the "How to's" of smart real estate investing **$10.95**

THE BEST OF BOB BRUSS
by Robert Bruss

This book is a compilation of the best columns written by Bob Bruss over the years on all facets of real estate. His columns are published in hundreds of papers across the country every week. Lean on his experience **$24.95**

AVOIDING THE DUE ON SALE CLAUSE—BOOK
by Robert Bruss

Mr. Bruss offers his insights as a real estate investment expert and a licensed attorney about how you can deal with the due-on-sale clause . . . Book **$12.00**
A Two Hour tape is also available **$12.00**

CRISIS REAL ESTATE INVESTING
by Hal Morris

The 5-year plan to increase and protect your assets from potential disaster **$14.95**

ZERO DOWN DEALS—WORKING WITH YOUR REALTOR
by Steve Thomas

One of the nation's top "Zero-Down" experts explains how you can teach your Realtor to negotiate zero down deals for you **$29.95**

HOW TO MAKE THE REAL ESTATE CRASH GO BOOM

by Steve Thomas

A leading national real estate expert teaches you the fine art of using a weak economy to your financial advantage **$19.95**

OVERCOMING NEGATIVE CASH FLOWS

by David Shamy

A situation every active real estate investor finds himself in, negative cash flow can be a problem in your past after studying the techniques outlined in this book **$24.95**

LANDLORDING, A PIECE OF CAKE

by David Shamy

Are you a landlord? Would you like to be? Do you hesitate because of the hassle involved? Don't hesitate, David Shamy's methods for landlording will help you eliminate almost every problem you could encounter before it happens **$24.95**

NOTHING DOWN

by Robert G. Allen

The great national best seller. A thorough exploration of ingenius financing techniques. A highly recommended book for the beginning and experienced investor alike **$13.95**

HOW TO WAKE UP THE FINANCIAL GENIUS INSIDE YOU

by Mark O. Haroldsen

A pioneer in the field of real estate investing Mr. Haroldsen shows how he did it. Facts and stories that come alive. If you want excitement this book must be read **$10.95**

About the Author

Wade B. Cook started investing in real estate in the late 70s. While working with the real estate investment models that others were promoting as the key to wealth, Wade developed his own working real estate investment formula which proved to be more conducive to today's tight money market.

In the spring of 1981, Wade decided to share his formula with the investment world and began lecturing throughout the country for two other giants in the business: Mark Haroldsen and Robert G. Allen.

Today, Mr. Cook is conducting seminars and conventions in all parts of the country. He is also author of several other books and investor help materials, which include: *How to Buy Real Estate Tax Benefits, Cook's Book on Creative Real Estate, How to Pick up Foreclosures, Owner Financing, The Three Entity Approach to Investing in Real Estate, a Total Property Record Keeping System,* a functional set of Legal Forms and taped seminars on various subjects.

If you'd like a copy of Mr. Cook's speaking schedule, please write Investment and Tax Publications at P.O. Box 1201-M, Orem, Utah, 84057 or call 1-801-224-3500.